P

Life in a
FLOWERBED

Clare Oliver

RAINTREE
STECK-VAUGHN
PUBLISHERS

A Harcourt Company

Austin   New York
www.raintreesteckvaughn.com

Published by Raintree Steck-Vaughn Publishers, an imprint of Steck-Vaughn Company.

Project Editors: Sean Dolan and Tamsin Osler
Production Manager: Richard Johnson
Illustrated by Stuart Lafford and Tim Haywood
Designed by Ian Winton

Planned and produced by Discovery Books

Library of Congress Cataloging-in-Publication Data

Oliver, Clare.
Life in a flowerbed/Clare Oliver.
p.cm. -- (Microhabitats)
Includes bibliographical references (p.).
ISBN 0-7398-4329-X
1. Garden ecology--Juvenile literature. 2. Beds (Gardens)--Juvenile literature.
[1. Garden ecology. 2.Ecology.] I. Title.

QH541.5.G37 O44 2001
577.5'54--dc21

2001019551

Printed and bound in the United States
1 2 3 4 5 6 7 8 9 LB 07 06 05 04 03 02

Acknowledgments
The publishers would like to thank the following for permission to reproduce their pictures:
Cover: Bruce Coleman Collection; p.6t: Geoff Kidd/Oxford Scientific Films; p.6b: Robert P. Carr/Bruce Coleman;
p.10: Dan Griggs/NHPA; p.11: N.A. Callow/NHPA; p.12: K.G. Prestom-Mafham/Premaphotos Wildlife; p.13: Chris
Fairclough Picture Library; p.14: J. Brackenbury/Bruce Coleman; p.15: Tim Shepherd/Oxford Scientific Films; p.16: G.J.
Cambridge/NHPA; p.18: Michael Leach/Oxford Scientific Films; p.20: Stephen Dalton/NHPA; p.21: Kim Taylor/Bruce
Coleman; p.22: N.A. Callow/NHPA; p.23t: Martin Garwood/NHPA; p.23b: J. Brackenbury/Bruce Coleman; p.24t: John
Shaw/NHPA; p.24b: Jane Burton/Bruce Coleman; p.25: Photodisc; p.26t: Alberto Nardi/NHPA; p.26b:
Kim Taylor/Bruce Coleman; p.27: Chris Fairclough/Discovery Picture Library; p.28:
Hans Reinhard/Bruce Coleman; p.29: Joe Blossom/NHPA.

Contents

The Living Flowerbed

The Flowerbed

Every flowerbed, whether it's in a garden or a public park, is an amazing microhabitat. Most of the plants that live there have been planted and cared for by a gardener. They may have been chosen for their color or delicious scent. Other life forms that live in or visit the flowerbed include weeds, insects, and songbirds.

To a certain extent, gardeners can select these inhabitants, too. They can grow **species** of flowers that attract butterflies and bees, and plant shrubs with berries that attract birds. They can also do various things to limit the growth of weeds.

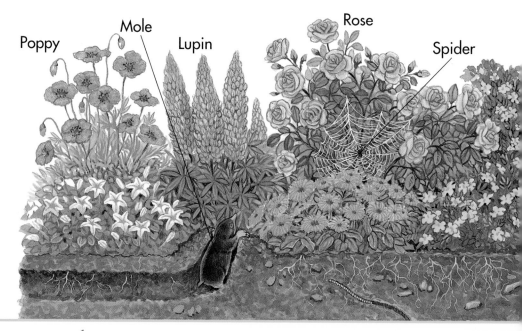

Poppy · Mole · Lupin · Rose · Spider

Sun or Shade

No two flowerbeds are the same. Different soils and conditions, such as weather, nearby buildings, and even traffic, can affect the plants and wildlife that live in the flowerbed. So does what is planted nearby. If a neighboring tree blocks out the light, only plants that like shade will flourish in the bed.

A flowerbed constantly changes. In summer, it teems with life. In winter, flowers and leaves die back, and the plants remain dormant until spring.

Guess What?

The flowers of the nasturtium plant are rich in Vitamin C and iron. They were once used as a remedy against scurvy, a disease caused by lack of Vitamin C.

Gardeners can grow specific plants to encourage the predators of garden pests. Roses, sunflowers, and French marigolds attract hoverflies and lacewings, while nettles attract ladybugs. All feed on aphids, which can harm flowers.

The scents of specific flowers have special properties. Lavender is relaxing and is sometimes dried and stuffed into "sleep pillows."

Red admiral

Buddleia

Thrush

Bee

Worm

Hosta

Shapes and Colors

There are thousands of different kinds of flowers. Some sway alone on a single stem like the tulip and poppy, while others form spires (lupins and delphiniums) or umbrella-shaped clusters (candytuft). Petals may form bowl shapes or pompoms, trumpets, or bells.

Standing Tall

Gardeners often plant taller flowers at the back of the bed and shorter plants at the front. The tallest

ones stand over a yard (1 m) high and need strong, thick stems to support them. Tall flowers include delphiniums, lupins, and foxgloves. Mid-sized flowers include poppies and geraniums, while tiny pinks, crocuses, and alpine plants stay close to the ground, out of the wind.

Plant Life Cycles

Some flowering plants have a life cycle of only one growing season. They produce seeds just once and then die. These plants are called annuals. Plants that live for two growing seasons are called biennials. Perennial plants produce seeds for at least three years.

Seeds, Bulbs, and Tubers

Flowering plants grow from seeds, bulbs, or tubers. Bulbs and tubers are underground thickened stems that store food to nourish the plant, especially during cold or very dry weather.

A flowerbed planted with spring flowers: red tulips and white hyacinths (foreground), and white narcissi and grape hyacinths (background).

How Plants Grow

In spring, sunshine and water trigger the plant to produce roots and shoots. The first root soon becomes a tangle that sucks up water and **nutrients** from the soil. Shoots push up to the surface, and leaves unfurl to collect light from the Sun.

1.   2.   3.   4.

1. This seed is about to germinate. 2. The outer case of the seed has broken open. 3. A root grows down to anchor the new plant in the soil. 4. The first leaves begin to grow.

See for Yourself

Grow a miniature flowerbed in a window box. Spell out your name in your flowerbed. Scratch the letters in the bare soil with a stick. Then put in some candytuft seeds and sprinkle over with soil. Keep the box moist, but not too wet, and wait for the flowers to grow.

Pollination

A flower is pollinated when the stigma or female reproductive organ of a flower is brushed with the powdery **pollen** made by the stamens (male reproductive organs) of the same type. The pollen may be carried by the wind, an insect, or an animal. Once a flower is fertilized, its ovary can produce a seed.

Some flowers have female or male parts only. Others, like the lily, have both male and female parts.

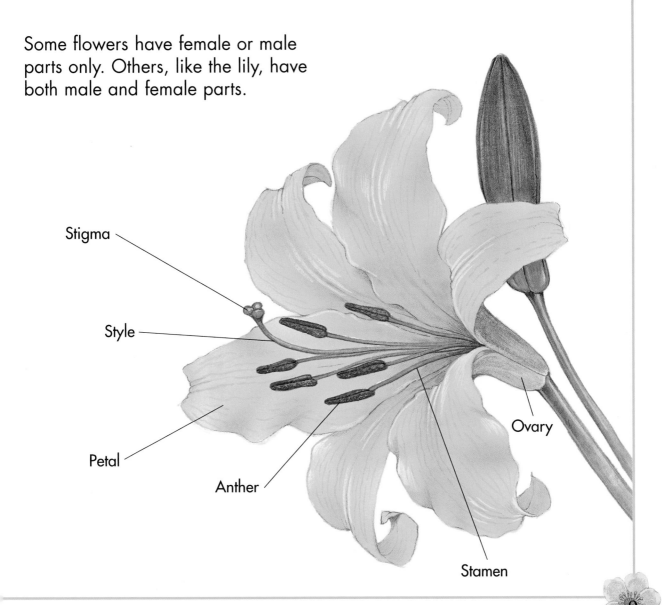

Stigma

Style

Petal

Anther

Ovary

Stamen

The Soil

Kinds of Soil

The soil in the flowerbed provides the moisture and nutrients the plants need. The soil may be chalky or sandy, crumbly or clay-like. Different plants prefer different kinds of soil.

Millipedes like moist soil and feed on decaying vegetation. Gardeners consider them pests because they can damage seedlings and soft shoots.

Gardeners can improve, or fertilize, the soil by mixing in manure or compost, a soil-like material of well-rotted vegetable and plant matter. They can also cover it with a mulch, such as a layer of bark chippings or cocoa pods. Mulching helps keep in moisture and helps stop the growth of weeds.

Natural Helpers

Earthworms, pill bugs, millipedes, and mites feed on decaying leaves and animal matter in the soil. These tiny creatures break up the soil as they tunnel through it, which also allows nutrients to be spread more easily through the soil. The creatures' own waste is a natural compost, too.

Pill bugs are usually found in dark, damp places. They are night hunters and feed mainly on plant material.

Fungi and bacteria also help matter decompose, or rot, in the soil. This allows plant roots to spread through the soil easily and rainwater to drain.

Guess What?

Pill bugs and sow bugs, which are also known as woodlice, are not insects, like beetles, but a type of crustacean, like a crab.

A type of Australian earthworm can grow to 11 feet (3.3 m) in length!

Worms can survive being cut in two, but it is not true that they do not feel pain.

Food Farms

Ants often make their nests in soil. The ants feed on honeydew, a sticky, sugary substance produced by **aphids**, which are tiny insects about the size of the head of a pin. The ants "farm" the aphids like cattle, fighting off their **predators** and "milking" them for a sugary substance called honeydew. Although ants do not damage plants in the flowerbed, aphids can do serious damage to plants. Ants actually help plants by adding air to the soil when they tunnel.

These red ants are tending to bean aphids. Ants encourage aphids to secrete honeydew by "tickling" them with their antennae.

Slimy Trails

Slugs and snails are both **gastropods**, and have a single muscle-like foot. Their soft bodies are almost identical, except that snails carry a shell on their back. They belong to the **mollusk** group of animals.

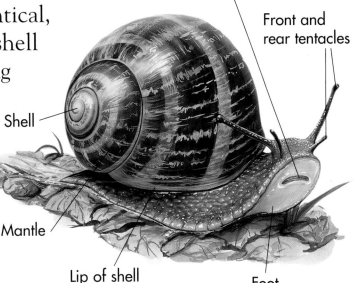

Mouth and rasping tongue

Front and rear tentacles

Shell

Mantle

Lip of shell

Foot

Both slugs and snails can devastate a flowerbed. Their favorite flowery feasts include hostas (a type of lily) and tulips, but just about any soft, fleshy plant matter will do.

Slugs and snails harm leaves by scraping them with their rasping tongue and depositing a sticky slime.

Guess What?

An ant's nest may contain more than 100,000 ants.

Ants may bite in self-defense. Some species even spit out acid.

Like the snail, the slug also has a shell. The slug's shell is soft and found under the surface of its skin.

Slugs and snails may lay as many as 200 eggs at a time.

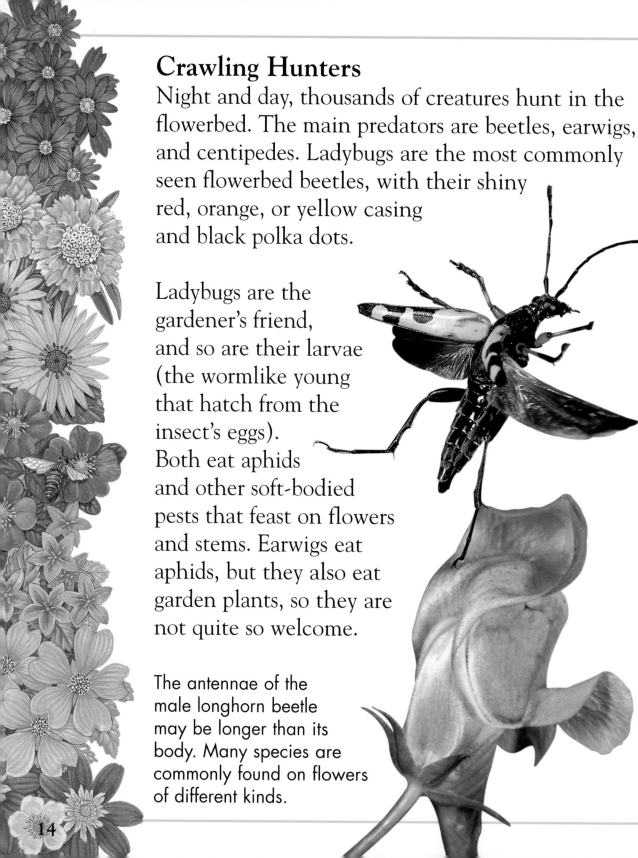

Crawling Hunters

Night and day, thousands of creatures hunt in the flowerbed. The main predators are beetles, earwigs, and centipedes. Ladybugs are the most commonly seen flowerbed beetles, with their shiny red, orange, or yellow casing and black polka dots.

Ladybugs are the gardener's friend, and so are their larvae (the wormlike young that hatch from the insect's eggs). Both eat aphids and other soft-bodied pests that feast on flowers and stems. Earwigs eat aphids, but they also eat garden plants, so they are not quite so welcome.

The antennae of the male longhorn beetle may be longer than its body. Many species are commonly found on flowers of different kinds.

Underground

Beneath the soil, soldier beetle larvae and centipedes wriggle about in search of **prey** to feed on. Centipedes, which have amazingly powerful jaws, prefer to hunt at night. Centipedes are not insects because they don't have six legs. They don't have 100 legs either, despite their name.

Guess What?

Soldier beetles get their name from their red and black coloring, which makes them look like they're wearing a military uniform!

Centipedes shed their skin as they grow.

Earwigs are very protective mothers. They lick their eggs clean and guard them from predators.

Life on a Plant

Bugs

Many people call all creepy-crawly little creatures "bugs." In fact, bugs are a specific kind of insect that has a beak for sucking up liquids such as plant juices—or blood! Sap-sucking bugs include whiteflies and common aphids (commonly known as greenflies). Gardeners consider them pests because they suck up the juice of leaves, stems, and flowers. Sap-sucking insects can spread plant viruses from one flower to another. The disease may cause mottling or distortion of leaves and poor growth.

Sap-sucking bugs have long tubes through which they suck up plant and animal juices.

Jumping Bugs

Most bugs have wings, but some are also excellent jumpers, such as froghoppers, leafhoppers, and spittlebugs. You might not see their speedy leaps, but you are sure to spot the spittlebugs' larvae, or at least the frothy "cuckoo spit" where they hide and keep their soft bodies safe and wet.

Guess What?

An aphid can produce 50 grubs in a week. Within seven days all will have grown to adulthood and be ready to breed.

Shield bugs are often known as stink bugs because they ward off predators by producing a disgusting smell!

The bug family includes the world's loudest insects, cicadas, which create their distinctive "song" by vibrating membranes on their abdomen.

Shield bugs get their name from the shape of their bodies.

Web Weavers

On a dewy morning, you can often see glistening webs that have been spun between plants in the flowerbed. These are spun by orb weaver spiders as a sticky net to entrap flies and other prey in mid-air. The web is not sticky enough to hold the prey for long, so the spider lies in wait, ready to attack. It paralyzes the fly with a poisonous bite and wraps it in its silken threads.

The most common webs are round orb webs. They have to be spun each day, or at least repaired.

Making a Web

1. The spider spins a bridge between two points.

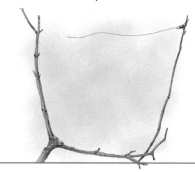

2. The spider drops down to attach one of the bridge threads to a point below.

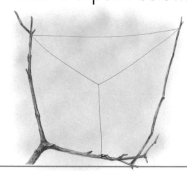

Spider Features

Spiders are not insects, because they have eight legs. They belong to a group of animals called **arachnids**. All spiders are hunters, but not all spiders spin webs. Wolf spiders outrun their prey, while jumping spiders leap at their victim.

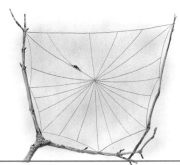

Guess What?

When silk first comes out of the spider's spinnerets, it is still runny. It sets in the air.

The male ladybug spider is less than a quarter of the size of his mate!

Crab spiders can camouflage themselves by gradually changing their color to that of the flower petals where they lurk. It normally takes them 4 or 5 days to change back to their original color.

3. It adds threads around the edge of the web and into the center.

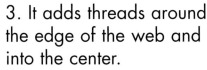

4. It makes a tight spiral in the web center and adds sticky threads to catch prey.

On the Wing

Stripes for Danger

In summer, a flowerbed may contain plentiful food for bees. Most flowers are pollinated by honeybees or their larger, plumper relatives, the bumblebees (right). Like ants, honeybees live together in colonies. The female workers fetch pollen and nectar, the sugary liquid inside a flower, for the larvae and "dance" by making a pattern of movements to tell other bees where there's food! The nectar is turned into sweet, syrupy honey.

Spot the Difference

The honeybee is not very furry, for a bee. Its stripes are duller than a wasp's.

Wasps are longer and more slender than bees. Their shiny bodies are not as furry, either.

Wasps

Both bees and wasps can give a nasty sting in self-defense. Like bees, many wasps are striped. Yellow jackets, also known as common wasps, feed on sugary nectar. In other ways, though, bees and wasps are quite different. Wasps feed their grubs (young) on caterpillars and have longer, more slender bodies. "Hornet" is the common name for several larger kinds of wasp.

The wasps inside this nest are tending to the larvae and eggs inside their cells.

Stand very still if you are watching bees or wasps, and don't get too close. They can give you a painful sting.

See for Yourself

If you see a wasp crawling slowly over a wooden fence, it's probably a paper wasp or a yellow jacket. These wasps chew up wood into a papery pulp, which they use to build their nest.

Take a pipe cleaner and gently brush it against the stamens of a flower, then check it for pollen. See how a bee's legs pick up pollen?

21

Fluttering Flies

Many flowerbed flies wear a sneaky disguise. The hoverfly's black and yellow coloring makes it look just like a yellow jacket, and so other insects keep away, fearing a sting. Thick-headed flies use the same trick, though some look more like bees than wasps. These flies are busiest during the day, when flowers are fully open.

Flowers attract pollinating insects like this hoverfly with bright flowers, special markings, or a strong scent.

Losing Legs

At twilight, lacewings and craneflies (right) come out to feed. Normally, long, gangly craneflies have six legs, but they often lose one or two in a spider's web. Craneflies do not live very long as adults, but they may survive for years underground as larvae, or leatherjackets. Leatherjackets are flowerbed pests, eating the roots of precious plants.

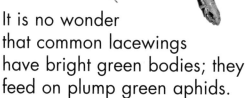

It is no wonder that common lacewings have bright green bodies; they feed on plump green aphids. They get their name because of their see-through, lacy wings.

Guess What?

There are about 15,000 different species of cranefly. Craneflies even lived in prehistoric times.

Thick-headed fly larvae are not very polite. Eggs are laid on the body of a bee, wasp, or other host. The grubs burrow into the host's body and eat it from the inside out!

Honey guides are markings on a flower, like runway lights on an airstrip. They guide insects toward the pollen.

23

Beautiful Butterflies

Caterpillars are the grubs (young) of butterflies or moths. They hungrily munch their way through leaves and stems, causing a lot of damage in the flowerbed.

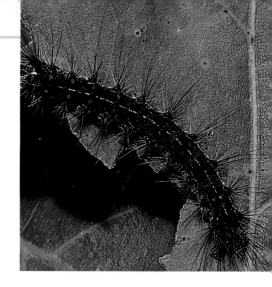

Once they have changed into butterflies or moths (a process called metamorphosis), they benefit flowering plants when they visit a flowerbed and sip nectar from the plants with their long, tube-like mouth. They pick up pollen on their wings and as they move on to other flowers, these are pollinated and seeds can begin to grow.

A comma butterfly pupates in its chrysalis.

Great Attractors

Gardeners often plant nectar-rich, scented flowers to attract butterflies. Flowers of this kind include lavender, lilac, honeysuckle, sweet william, and, of course, the butterfly bush (buddleia).

Guess What?

Butterflies and moths shimmer when light reflects from the tiny scales that cover their wings.

Butterflies differ from true flies in that they have two pairs of wings, not one.

Most moth caterpillars spend the pupa stage (the sleeplike state between caterpillar and moth) inside a silken cocoon, whereas butterflies pupate in a shiny chrysalis.

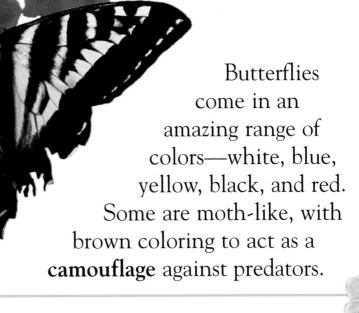

There are some 500 species of swallowtail worldwide. Most species have little "tails" on their rear wings.

Butterflies come in an amazing range of colors—white, blue, yellow, black, and red. Some are moth-like, with brown coloring to act as a **camouflage** against predators.

25

Garden Birds

All sorts of birds visit the flowerbed, especially in spring and summer. Thrushes, starlings, and robins dig for juicy worms, using a keen sense of hearing to know just where to strike. They eat fruit and berries, too.

Other insect-eating birds include swifts, warblers, and woodpeckers. They benefit the flowerbed by reducing the numbers of aphids, caterpillars, and other plant-eating pests.

Pigeons (above) feed on seeds, berries, and other fruits, as well as worms and insects, whereas thrushes (below) feed on worms, insects, berries, and even fruit.

Feeding the Birds

In autumn, small garden birds like chickadees, finches, and titmice often come to the garden to feed on plants with seeds or berries, such as rose hips. In winter, you can attract them by putting up a hanging bird feeder filled with seeds, nuts, and different grains.

Finches, nuthatches, and chickadees are attracted to hanging bird feeders.

See for Yourself

Natural bird food is scarce in winter. Put out piles of different seeds and see which bird eats what. Leave a dish of water, too, for the birds to drink and bathe in. But be careful to place them out of reach of cats!

Put lots of seeds, nuts, and raisins in a bowl. Ask an adult to pour melted lard or fat over it and then mix it all together. When the bird cake is cool, cut slices for the birds. Why not add pieces of apple or bacon strips to the mix?

Borrow a birdsong tape from your local library and learn to identify garden visitors by ear alone.

Other Visitors

Furry Creatures

When small mammals visit the flowerbed, they can cause a lot of damage. Moles (below) tunnel underground for juicy worms. They are expert diggers, with shovel-shaped front paws that are perfect for the job. Unfortunately, they leave messy piles of soil around, damage plants, and greatly reduce the worm population. Squirrels dig, too, especially for tender bulbs. In late summer, you might even spot a shy field mouse in a flowerbed, attracted by all the seeds and berries.

Lying in Wait

A visiting fox might nap among the foliage of the plants in a flowerbed. The sheltered bed also hides cats waiting to pounce on birds or mice. Some gardeners use sprays or scarecrows to try to keep mammal pests away from their flowerbeds.

The harvest mouse is an expert climber. It feeds on seeds, grasses, and parts of flowers.

See for Yourself

Winter is the best time to spot signs of mammal visitors. Look for these footprints in the snow:

Raccoon

Squirrel

Rabbit

Fox

Glossary

Aphids Small, soft-bodied insects, such as the greenfly. Aphids are bugs. They have a beak-like mouth for piercing plant stems and sucking up plant sap (juice).

Arachnids Animals that have eight legs and two parts to their body. Spiders, scorpions, and mites are all types of arachnid.

Beetles Insects with strong jaws for biting. An adult beetle's wings are protected by hard, shiny wing cases.

Bugs Insects that feed only on liquids, using a beak-like mouth to pierce and suck. An adult bug's wings cross over on its back to make an "X" shape.

Camouflage Coloring, or a means of disguise, that makes an animal blend in with its surroundings so that it is more difficult for predators to see.

Fertilize To make something able to produce fruit, seeds, or offspring.

Gastropods Mollusks that have a large, muscle-like foot for moving along on. Snails and slugs are both gastropods.

Grubs Insect babies that look nothing like their parents. Adult insects have three parts to their body and six legs, but grubs are worm-like and may have no legs at all.

Larva An insect baby, such as a beetle grub, that does not resemble its parent.

Mammals Warm-blooded animals, such as foxes or mice, that give birth to live young and feed them on mother's milk.

Microhabitat A small, specialized place, such as a flowerbed or a freshwater pond, where particular animals live and plants grow.

Mollusks Boneless animals with soft bodies that need to be kept damp and are sometimes protected by a shell. Snails, mussels, and octopuses are all types of mollusk.

Nutrients The minerals and other substances in soil that nourish or feed a plant and help it to grow.

Pollen A powder produced by the male parts of a flower. Pollen is usually yellow. For a plant to be fertilized and able to produce a seed, pollen has to be brushed against its female parts.

Predators Animals that hunt other animals for food.

Prey Animals that are hunted by other animals for food.

Species A type of animal or plant; for example, the wood ant is a species of ant.

Thick-headed flies There are about 1,000 species of thick-headed fly. They belong to a different family than hoverflies, although both have wasp-like markings.

Tubers Swollen underground roots or stems. Tubers can produce tiny buds that will eventually grow into new plants. Flowers that grow from tubers include dahlias and irises.

Weeds Plants that grow wild. Gardeners try to get rid of weeds because they use up nutrients and water in the soil. They can also strangle other plants or block out their light.

Further Reading

Morris, Karyn. *The Kids Can Press Jumbo Book of Gardening*. NY: Kids Can Pr, 2000.

Pupeza, Lori Kinstad. *How-To Gardening for Kids*. Minneapolis, MN: Abdo & Daughters, 2001.

Rosen, Michael J. *Down to Earth: Garden Secrets! Garden Stories! Garden Projects You Can Do!* NY: Harcourt Brace, 1998.

Rushing, Felder. *New Junior Garden Book*. NY: Better Homes and Gardens Books, 1999.

Index